Explore
the
Northeast

John Perritano

PICTURE CREDITS

Cover © Alan Schein Photography/Corbis; title page © Paul Conklin/PhotoEdit, Inc.; pages 2-3 © John Lawrence/Stone/Getty Images; pages 6-7, 25 (bottom right) © Digital Vision/Getty Images; pages 8, 35-e © Peter Barrett/Masterfile; pages 9, 34-b © Jeremy Woodhouse/Photodisc Red/Getty Images; pages 10, 11, 16 (inset), 16-17 (background), 19, 22, 25 (top right and bottom left), 28 (bottom), 31 (center left), 35-d, 35-f © The Granger Collection, NY; pages 12-13 (top), 30, 34-f © Lynda Richardson/Corbis; pages 12 (bottom), 30 (bottom), 35-c © John Burwell/ Foodpix/Getty Images; pages 13 (right), 34-c © Free Agents Limited/Corbis; pages 14, 31 (top left) © Ron Watts/Corbis; page 15 © Bob Krist/Corbis; page 18 © New York Historical Society, New York, USA/Bridgeman Art Library; pages 20, 34-a © North Wind/North Wind Picture Archives; page 23 © Andy Olenick; pages 26 (bottom), 34-d © Sylvain Grandadam/Getty Images; pages 26-27 © Sekai Bunka/Premium/Panoramic Images; page 28 (top) © Bill Ross/Corbis; page 29 (bottom) © SuperStock; page 29 (inset) © Duomo/Corbis; page 31 (top right) © Gail Mooney/Masterfile; pages 31 (center right), 35-a © Eric Fowke/PhotoEdit, Inc.; page 31 (bottom left) © Garry Black/Masterfile; page 31 (bottom right) © Jim Erickson/Corbis; page 32 © Lake County Museum/Corbis; page 33 (left) *The Northeast* by Elspeth Leacock © 2002 National Geographic Society, photo © David Ball/The Stock Market; page 33 (center) *The Northeast: Its History and People* by Gare Thompson © 2003 National Geographic Society, photos (top) © The Granger Collection, New York, (bottom) © Tony Stone Images; page 33 (right) *The Northeast Today* © 2004 National Geographic Society, photo © Robert Harding/Digital Vision/Getty Images; page 36 © Dennis Curran/Index Stock.

Produced through the worldwide resources of the National Geographic Society, John M. Fahey, Jr., President and Chief Executive Officer; Gilbert M. Grosvenor, Chairman of the Board; Nina D. Hoffman, Executive Vice President and President, Books and Education Publishing Group.

PREPARED BY NATIONAL GEOGRAPHIC SCHOOL PUBLISHING

Ericka Markman, Senior Vice President and President, Children's Books and Education Publishing Group; Steve Mico, Senior Vice President, Editorial Director, Publisher; Francis Downey, Executive Editor; Richard Easby, Editorial Manager; Anne Stone, Lori Dibble Collins, Editors; Bea Jackson, Director of Layout and Design; Jim Hiscott, Design Manager; Cynthia Olson, Art Director; Margaret Sidlosky, Illustrations Director; Matt Wascavage, Manager of Publishing Services; Sean Philpotts, Production Manager; Ted Tucker, Production Specialist.

MANUFACTURING AND QUALITY CONTROL

Christopher A. Liedel, Chief Financial Officer; Phillip L. Schlosser, Director; Clifton M. Brown III, Manager

CONSULTANT AND REVIEWER

Sam Goldberger, emeritus professor, Capital Community College, Hartford, Connecticut.

BOOK DESIGN/PHOTO RESEARCH

Steve Curtis Design, Inc.

◄ Small towns like this one line
the coast of the Northeast.

Contents

Published by the National Geographic Society
1145 17th Street N.W.
Washington, D.C. 20036-4688

ISBN: 9780792254577
2016 2017 2018
5 6 7 8 9 10 11 12 13 14 15
Printed in the USA
RR Donnelley, Menasha, WI

Five Regions

The United States is a large country. It has 50 states. These states can be broken into five **regions.** The five regions are the Northeast, the Southeast, the Midwest, the Southwest, and the West.

A region is an area, such as a group of states, with something in common. Each region has its own history and kinds of land. Each region has its own **culture,** or way of life. In this book, you will read about the Northeast region.

region – an area, such as a group of states, with something in common

culture – a way of life

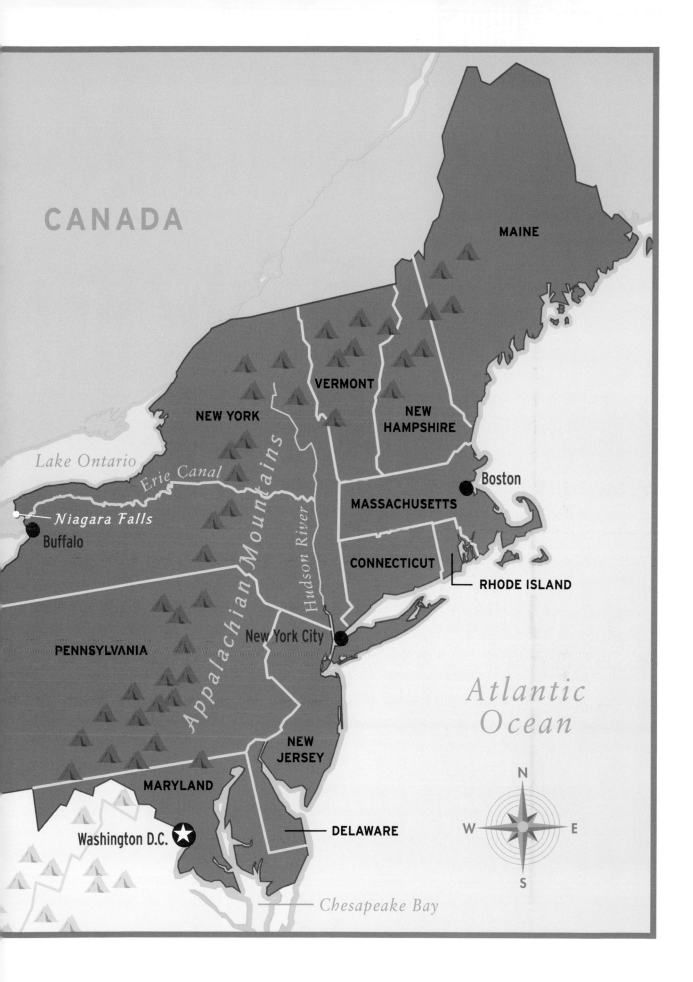

CANADA

MAINE

VERMONT

NEW YORK

NEW HAMPSHIRE

Lake Ontario

Erie Canal

Appalachian Mountains

Hudson River

Boston

MASSACHUSETTS

Niagara Falls

Buffalo

CONNECTICUT

RHODE ISLAND

New York City

PENNSYLVANIA

Atlantic Ocean

NEW JERSEY

MARYLAND

DELAWARE

N
W   E
S

Washington D.C.

Chesapeake Bay

Big Idea
The Northeast is shaped by its geography, history, economy, and people.

Set Purpose
Read to learn about life in the Northeast.

Welcome to the Northeast

Questions You Will Explore

Why is water important to the Northeast?

Why do people come to the Northeast?

The Northeast has 11 states. The states stretch from Maine to Maryland. The Northeast is the smallest region in the United States. Yet many big cities are found here. One of these cities is the capital of the United States. The region also has a long and important history. The city of Boston dates back to colonial times. The Northeast has mountains, too. People come to ski and snowboard here. What else does the Northeast have?

▼ Boston is one of several large cities in the Northeast.

▲ **Hikers enjoy the Appalachian Trail.**

The Appalachian Mountains

The Appalachian Mountains are found in the
Northeast. These mountains are very old. They are
some of the oldest mountains in the United States.
Forests cover most of these mountains. A trail
runs through the mountains. It is called the
Appalachian Trail. The trail is 2,144 miles long.
People like to hike on the trail. You can follow
the trail from Maine all the way to Georgia.

▲ The coast of Maine has many rocky cliffs.

The Atlantic Coast

Most states in the Northeast border the Atlantic Ocean. Boulders and jagged cliffs line the **coast** of Maine. Farther south, there are sandy beaches. Many **tourists** come to vacation on these beaches. They visit the shores of New Jersey, Delaware, and Maryland.

coast – the land at the edge of an ocean

tourist – a visitor to a place

▲ Whaling was a dangerous but important business in the 1800s.

Hunting for Whales

In the 1800s, **whaling** was a big business. Men hunted whales off the Northeast coast and far out to sea. Whaling ships set sail from ports in Massachusetts. They also sailed from Connecticut and Rhode Island. Whaling was hard work. Sailors sometimes stayed at sea for years. But the work was important. People needed whale oil for many things. For example, they used it to light their homes.

....

whaling – hunting for whales

▲ Textile mills brought money and jobs to the Northeast.

Working in Factories

The Northeast has many rivers. In the 1800s, people built factories by these rivers. The rushing water powered the factories. Many of the factories were **textile mills**. These mills turned cotton and wool into cloth. People used the cloth to make clothes and other goods. Many people moved to the Northeast for jobs in the mills.

textile mill – a factory where cloth is made

Economy

▶ A waterman checks his catch of crabs on the Chesapeake Bay.

Living Off the Sea

The fishing **industry** is important in the Northeast. It brings money and jobs. People catch fish, lobsters, and crabs. This is how they make a living. The Chesapeake Bay is one place where people fish. Native Americans called the bay the "great **shellfish** bay." Today, watermen harvest crabs, oysters, and clams in these waters.

industry – a large-scale business

shellfish – a sea creature with a shell

12

▲ **Wall Street in New York City is a center of world commerce.**

The Business of Money

The Northeast is a center of **commerce**. Commerce is the buying and selling of things. The Northeast also has many banks. These banks help companies from around the world. Banks help them borrow and save money. Banks keep businesses strong.

....
commerce – the buying and selling of things

13

▲ **Washington, D.C., is the capital of the United States.**

Bright Lights, Big Cities

The Northeast is home to many large cities.
One of these cities is Washington, D.C. This
city is the nation's capital. The President of the
United States works here. So do many other
people in the government.

Another Northeast city is New York. More
than eight million people live in New York City.
It is the biggest city in the United States. New
York City is also home to the Statue of Liberty.

▲ Northeast cities have many famous museums.

City Life

The Northeast has many museums and theaters. Some of these are among the world's best. People come from far away to visit. They come to enjoy the city culture.

The Northeast is known for its cities and much more. It has beaches and water. It has mountains and trails. It has a rich history, too. Come to the Northeast and see for yourself!

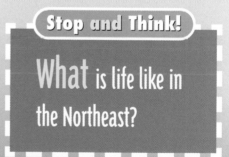

Stop and Think!

What is life like in the Northeast?

15

Recap

Describe what life is like in the Northeast.

Set Purpose

Discover how a canal shaped the Northeast.

▶ **DeWitt Clinton**

The Erie Canal

In the early 1800s, many people left the Northeast. They moved west to settle on farms. Traveling west was hard. There were few roads. There were no trains. People could not go all the way by boat.

A man named DeWitt Clinton had an idea. He decided to build a **canal.** The canal would stretch from the Hudson River to Lake Erie. It would link two regions, the Northeast and the Midwest.

canal – a channel that is dug to connect two bodies of water

▼ Clinton dreamed of building a canal between Lake Erie and the Hudson River.

Work Begins

Many people thought Clinton's idea was silly. Some said it would not work. The canal would be 363 miles long! Mountains and forests were in the way.

Clinton proved them wrong. Work began on the canal on July 4, 1817. Workers dug the canal by hand. The first part took two years to finish! It linked two towns in New York. The towns were 15 miles apart.

▼ Workers dug the Erie Canal by hand.

▲ Crowds celebrated the opening of the Erie Canal.

The Canal Opens

Workers kept digging. Eight years later, they finished the canal. A grand opening was held to celebrate. It took place in New York City on November 4, 1825. On that day, the first boat arrived from Buffalo. DeWitt Clinton was on board.

Crowds gathered along the canal. When the boat passed, people cheered and waved flags. People could now travel easily between the Northeast and the Midwest.

Moving Boats Uphill

Part of the trip to Lake Erie was uphill. Some boats did not have motors. So teams of horses and mules walked beside the canal. They pulled each boat forward.

The canal also had a series of **locks.** A lock is like an elevator for a boat. After a boat enters the lock, a gate at one end swings closed. The lock fills with water. The boat rises. Then a gate at the other end opens to let the boat out.

lock – a part of a canal where boats can be raised or lowered to different water levels, using a system of gates

▼ **Horses pulled boats up the canal to locks.**

20

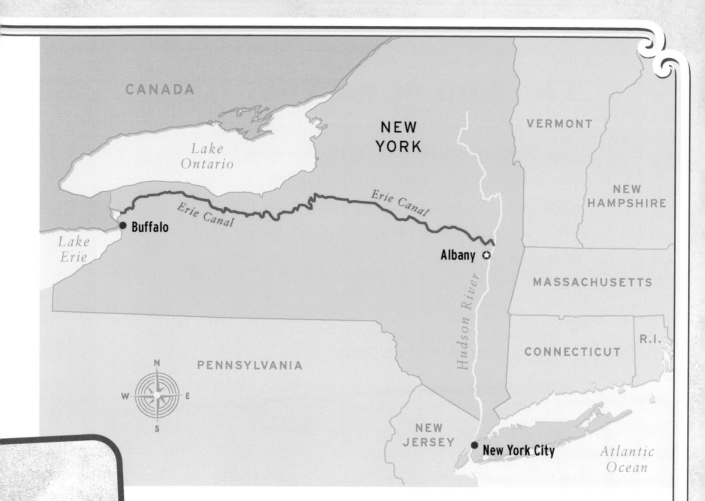

▲ The canal linked Lake Erie to the
Hudson River and New York City.

East and West

The Erie Canal became very popular. It was
the best way to travel west. It was also the
easiest way to bring goods east.

Thousands of travelers boarded boats
and headed west. Crops from the Midwest
were loaded into boats and shipped east.
Before long, New York City had the busiest
port in the country. Many boats loaded or
unloaded there.

The End of an Era

By the 1850s, times had changed. Railroads gave people new choices. Traveling by train was easy and fast. Trains could haul more goods, too. Fewer and fewer boats took the Erie Canal. It was no longer the best way to travel.

▼ Before long, train travel was faster and easier than taking the Erie Canal.

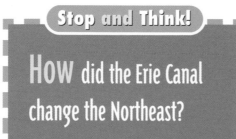
▲ People relax along the Erie Canal.

The Canal Today

Today, New York State has built parks and hiking trails along the canal. Some boats still use the canal. But they are just for fun. The Erie Canal is no longer used for transportation. Yet it played an important role in the history of the Northeast. The canal helped the region grow. It helped the country grow, too.

Stop and Think!

HOW did the Erie Canal change the Northeast?

Recap
Explain how the Erie Canal helped the Northeast.

Set Purpose
Read to learn more about the Northeast.

CONNECT WHAT YOU HAVE LEARNED

Explore the Northeast

The Northeast is the smallest region in the United States. Yet it is packed with people, history, and culture.

Here are some ideas that you learned about the Northeast region.

- Mountains and water are important to life in the Northeast.
- Factory towns grew up along the region's many rivers in the 1800s.
- In the mid-1800s, the Erie Canal was the main link between the Northeast and the Midwest.
- Many big cities are located in the Northeast.

Check What You Have Learned

HOW is the Northeast shaped by its land, history, economy, and people?

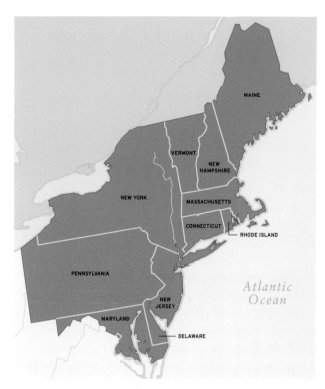

▲ The 11 states in the Northeast are near the Atlantic Ocean.

▲ Rivers once powered many factories.

▲ The Erie Canal was important to the economy of the Northeast.

▲ Boston is just one of many cities in the Northeast.

25

Awesome Falls

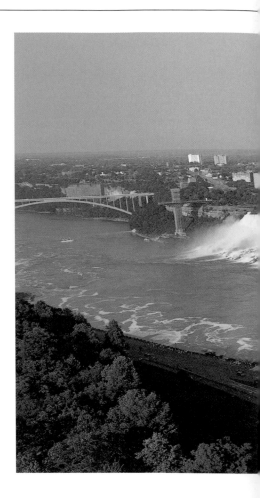

Niagara Falls is in western New York. It was formed 12,000 years ago by melting glaciers. Niagara Falls is actually two waterfalls. Both are huge. The water drops more than 170 feet to the river below.

One waterfall is in Canada. It is called Horseshoe Falls. The other waterfall is on the American side of the river. It is called the American Falls. Visitors can take a boat to see the falls up close.

▼ The Amish have a special way of life.

▼ One part of Niagara Falls is in New York. The other part is in Canada.

Amish Culture

The Amish are a group of people who believe in a simple way of life. They reject many modern things. The Amish do not own cars. Instead, they ride in horse-drawn buggies. The Amish do not watch TV or use computers. They believe in hard work and family time. The Amish originally came from Europe. Now, many Amish live in Pennsylvania. They are sometimes called the Pennsylvania Dutch.

▲ This is what Ellis Island looks like today.

Ellis Island

In the 1800s and early 1900s, millions of people left their homes in other countries. They came to live in the United States. Many of those immigrants passed through Ellis Island. Ellis Island is in New York Harbor. It is close to the Statue of Liberty.

More than 12 million immigrants entered the United States through Ellis Island. The island was called the Gateway to America. The island's buildings are now a museum.

▲ Immigrants waited in line at Ellis Island.

Snowboarding

Many people consider the Northeast the home of snowboarding. The first snowboarding competitions were held in Vermont in the 1970s.

A snowboard looks like a small surfboard. You ride it on snow. Mount Snow in Vermont's Green Mountains is one of the best places to snowboard.

▼ **The Green Mountains in Vermont are sometimes white with snow.**

Many kinds of words are used in this book. Here you will learn about compound words. You will also learn about possessives.

Compound Words

A compound word is made by joining two shorter words. You can often figure out what a compound word means by knowing what the two shorter words mean.

water + man = waterman

A **waterman** hauls in his daily catch.

shell + fish = shellfish

A crab is one kind of **shellfish.**

Possessives

A possessive is a word that shows ownership. It shows that something belongs to someone. Find the possessives below. Can you tell how they are formed?

The **nation's** capital is Washington, D.C.

The Northeast has some of the **world's** best theaters.

Many people thought **Clinton's** idea for a canal was silly.

A **canal's** locks help raise and lower boats.

The **region's** mountains are sometimes white with snow.

The **island's** buildings are now a museum.

Research and Write

Write About the Northeast

You read about the Northeast region. Now learn more about one of its states. Pick a state from the map on page 5. Find out what makes that state special. Then write a brochure to share what you have learned.

Research
Collect books and reference materials, or go online.

Read and Take Notes
As you read, take notes and draw pictures.

Write
Now write a brochure telling tourists about the state you have picked. What is the state best known for? Why should people come here to visit? Write about the state's geography, history, economy, and culture.

Read and Compare

Read More About the Northeast

Find and read other books about the Northeast. As you read, think about these questions.

- What influences have shaped this region?
- What makes this region special?
- How is this region important to the rest of the country?

Books to Read

▲ Take a guided tour through the states of the Northeast.

▲ Find out about the events and people that helped build the Northeast.

▲ Learn more about the culture and contributions of the Northeast.

Glossary

canal (page 17)
A channel that is dug to connect two bodies of water
The Erie Canal linked Lake Erie with the Hudson River.

coast (page 9)
The land at the edge of an ocean
Rocky cliffs are common along the coast of Maine.

commerce (page 13)
The buying and selling of things
Wall Street is the center of commerce in the United States.

culture (page 4)
A way of life
The Amish have a special culture.

industry (page 12)
A large-scale business
The fishing industry is important to the economy of the Northeast.

lock (page 20)
A part of a canal where boats can be raised or lowered to different water levels, using a system of gates
A series of locks was built into the Erie Canal.

region (page 4)
An area, such as a group of states, with something in common
The Northeast is one of five regions in the United States.

shellfish (page 12)
A sea creature with a shell
The waters along the coast are full of shellfish.

textile mill (page 11)
A factory where cloth is made
Many people worked in the textile mills.

tourist (page 9)
A visitor to a place
Many tourists to the Northeast spend time on the Appalachian Trail.

whaling (page 10)
Hunting for whales
Whaling was an important business in the Northeast in the 1800s.

Index